# Jesus Speaks

*A Narrative Poem*

by

# Philip Wesley Comfort

*Wipf & Stock*
PUBLISHERS
*Eugene, Oregon*

Wipf and Stock Publishers
199 West 8th Avenue, Suite 3
Eugene, Oregon 97401

Jesus Speaks
A Narrative Poem
By Comfort, Philip W
Copyright©2003 by Comfort, Philip Wesley
ISBN: 1-59244-653-1
Publication date 4/15/2004
Previously published by Feather Books, UK, 2003

# INTRODUCTION

A dramatic soliloquy such as <u>Jesus Speaks</u> really needs no introduction. The poem speaks for itself. Yet I hope the brief commentary I give will encourage anyone browsing the poem to look again.

It's a remarkable poem in many ways. First, it expresses as a soliloquy Jesus's innermost thoughts and experiences as he goes about his teaching and ministry. Second, Philip Comfort attempts what few poets have attempted to put down in verse: the inner spiritual struggle Jesus must have had as man realising that he had a divine dimension, that he had a growing direct contact with God his Father, that he had lived through the Creation, and that he was sent by his Father to redeem mankind. That, I believe, is the great achievement of this poem quite apart from its splendid poetical unfolding of Jesus's life as shown to us in the Gospels.

*John Waddington-Feather. Trinity 2003.*

# PROFILE

Philip W. Comfort, Ph. D., D. Litt. et Phil., has studied English Literature, Greek, and New Testament at the Ohio State University and the University of South Africa. He has taught these subjects at a number of colleges, including Wheaton College, Trinity Episcopal Seminary, Columbia International University, and Coastal Carolina University. He has written several books about the New Testament, in the fields of textual criticism, papyrology, and the Gospel of John, and is a published poet. He is co-editor of a volume entitled, <u>One Year Book of Poetry</u>, a collection of 365 Christian poems, with annotations.

He lives in Pawleys Island, South Carolina, with his wife Georgia. His three children (Jeremy, John, Peter) live nearby, as do his three grandchildren (Sage, Reid, Drake).

## PROLOGUE

night hangs a wintered moon
and since the brown crusted leaves
have all fallen
the bare-branched black elms
reaching to the cold-blue heavens
feel the depths
of frozen roots
and iced veins
as dead
but since rooted -
not moved -
brace against dark winds
and wait the parousia of spring
when the turned earth will flow again
and metamorphosis will come -
a brown chrysalis unfurling warm red wings.

# NARRATIVE

Devastated, dejected, recreant,
as if Roman-whipped and nailed,
they had not gone with him
to Calvary or even Galilee
as he (they forgot) foretold.
While the women moved
between the shades
moths to nightlight,
longing to touch any flame,
hoping for some flicker to kill the pain,
two of them deserted the rest
on a long sad walk to Emmaus.
"He was a potent prophet,
miraculous, messianic, and gifted."

      "But now they've done it,
those chief priests and rulers of ours,
they delivered him to Roman hands
who crucified our revolution."

      "We hoped he'd be the Redeemer,
our deliverer from onerous Caesar."

They didn't recognize him
as he himself drew near,
blind to his transfigured form
as he started to unveil:
"Oh, slow of heart to believe
all the prophets have spoken.
Shouldn't Christ suffer these things
before he entered into glory?
The story begins with prophet Moses
who wrote of the woman's seed
that would crush the serpent's head,

the same seed by Abraham sped
became the promised David
who like a grain of wheat died
and multiplies the earth with bread."

The two hung like ears upon a stalk
as they continued to walk with this stranger
and cling to his supernatural words:
"The Nazarene must have been the awaited One
in whom God could be seen and heard
without fear of death—the Lord God of Horeb
manifested meekly in Nazareth.
This was the one Isaiah foresaw
the Lord of glory become a tender plant
the stem of Jesse sprouting a fruit-filled Branch,
Immanuel of virgin birth, Wonderful from the womb,
mighty God, eternal Father, one and only Son,
rejected by his own who sliced the dayspring
before he could dawn in their sullen thoughts.
All this was written before about the Son of Man.
Their sanctuary has become a stumbling stone,
except to those who seek shelter from the wind.
There they'll find the selected Stone,
tried, tempered, tested to be sure
and now secured as God's foundation.
This is the One the builders rejected
and nailed as scrap to the tree.
But he whom they tried to make a grave
is raised headstone of the corner."
He made as if he'd go on further,
but they constrained him to join them
in the breaking of their bread,
which as he tore, glory broke -
he was quickly visible, then not -

the epiphany sealing its mark
in their glowing hearts
as they ran all the way back.
The women had hurried from the vault,
never thinking they'd be emptied of their gloom
by a flush of angels, an oracular rush:
 "Remember he told you three times and more
the Son of Man would be crushed and rise.
He is not here. You must go and tell them."
As they did, hope untombed their minds,
especially when Peter returned from despair
and said he had seen the risen One.
Just then, the others from Emmaus came,
but before they even mouthed a word
Jesus himself appeared more wonderous
than ashless phoenix  reborn,
more inspiring than lifted Lazarus,
born from death, the first, the best -
as spirit, as God, as flesh,
transfigured Godman, breather of their genesis.

Later, they gathered with others
on a Galilean hill flocked with elms
in a natural ampitheater
overlooking rippling waters.
There in the chill of spring dawn
under morning-gray clouds slowly coloring,
about five hundred came to see
if he had really risen, as had been said
by those who saw him in Jerusalem.
They wondered if this was ghost, phantom,
or hallucination of men denying crucifixion.
(Had they all forgotten his prophecy
that in three days he would part the grave

and appear to them in Gennesareth?)
He stood transformed before them,
divinely human, transfigured to effulgent form
with glorified body, transcending mind.
Some assembled there believed,
others doubted it was he,
supposing this was angel, supernatural,
or Elijah mystically come,
but not the risen Nazarene.
So the Prophet revealed his hands and side
and then unscrolled his poetic mind
to oracle the epic miracle
of his genesis, apocalypse, and exodus.

Raising his hands, he hushed the audience
and quietened their fierce minds.
Nothing could be heard but a few birdcaws
and aspen leafstalks clacking in the breeze,
as he began to slowly speak:
"When I was young I didn't know my origins.
These mysteries were kept from me,
but not His sweet secret presence
which I sensed in the thin winds,
in earth scents, raw wet wild.
Like you, I imbibed the verve of life,
breeze touching my skin was good
sun tanning my face felt right.
I savored the lingering tang
of newcut cypress for the carpenter shack,
threshed grain for mother's cooked bread,
fresh fish-catch fetched from Galilee
or further, from the western sea,
squashed grapes, must and wine.
I wandered the craggy hillsides

especially in verdant spring;
almond blossoms popping white,
pomegranates plumping on thin branches;
the curves, the crooked intrigued me:
gnarled olive trees, rumpled figs;
and the sounds, all the strains
were exotic symphonies:
honeybee hum, blackbird caw, sheep bleat,
rainfall, gurgling streams over brooked rocks.
I loved water, its changing colors in the sun,
its pure taste and feel on my sweaty face;
this liquid, so insubstantial and thin
gave life to all as much as air.

My town Nazareth was a broken branch
barely attached to Israel and hardly noticed.
Roman soldiers posted there for a time,
speaking Latin and bad Greek on our streets,
hacking broken Aramaic as they bartered for wine
and passed their time in nothing I could see.
This Gentile domination barbed our men
who'd whisper a coming Messiah,
as their eyes teared patriotic
and their songs extoled Jerusalem;
they thought some Maccabean might arise,
a warrior from the sunsoaked cliffs
to rid them of this pagan scourge.
Help would never come from Annas or Caiphas;
they were Caesar's friends, it was said,
more for Rome than our Jerusalem.
'When?' was the thought. 'Who?' was the sigh.
Some came and went, wafts and gusts,
Theudas, Judas the Galilean,
and many zealots chasing them.

Others abandoned Jerusalem
and went to the Dead Sea caves
to wait for the Prophet-Warrior-Prince.
But nothing changed and nothing could
until the wind shook the figs.
When I was old enough to understand,
father said we came from David's line
but we must keep this to ourselves
(we were fugitives of Herod's wrath).
He told me to study Hebrew and Torah
so I could divine God's word and will
and serve the Lord for Israel's good.
Each morning I entered our synagogue
cliffside to the Esdraelon Plain;
the breeze carried the scents of meadowlife:
apricot blossoms, ripening pomegranates,
into the synagogue of religion, and old minds
trying to decipher ancient letters
stroked on tawny parchment leaves.
At times I'd enter the scriptorium
cluttered with scrolls and smoky lamplight
by which scribes copied sheet after sheet,
the sacred solemn inscrutable writings,
making sure the text was transcribed as before
by the eminent rabbis and revered scholars
who formed the Tetragrammaton with holy awe,
intent on avoiding any error; as if they walked
on holy ground and YaHWeH himself was near,
for custom held (I was told) that no one ever knew
if Messiah in some jot or tittle might appear.

After I went to Passover for my barmitzvah,
I stayed behind in the temple courts
to discuss hard texts with men of letters

and questioned them about their hopes
for the long-awaited Redeemer.
I asked them how the Messiah
could be both David's root and shoot.
I questioned why David in spirit
called his Messiah 'my Lord'?
But they did not know the Revealer I knew,
only the words they thought He spoke.
The more we talked, the stronger I felt
that I was more than Abraham's heir.
I sensed I was both David' scion
and son of the glorious One.
This unearthly sense thickened in me all the more,
as when a candle burns, it fattens the stem
and when a cloud gets heavy, it begins to pour.
I startled the rabbis with wisdom not gotten from a book,
but from the ancient Apocalyptist, whose thoughts I knew.
As I journeyed home from Jerusalem
my spirit raced, my mind soared -
how could I tell anyone my sensation?
No one would comprehend or understand;
my knowledge would have to be enscrolled,
rolled up and sealed till a later time.
In the meanwhile, I continued to search the Scriptures
especially the prophetic scrolls
to discover why I wasn't in Jerusalem
or even in nearby Bethlehem,
homes of Israel's illustrious  kings.
Why had I become a Nazarene
so remote, obscure, removed.
Then the divine voice spoke again,
'You're David's root and David's shoot,
you're Branch, the Netzer - a Nazarene.
Only those with divine rootings

will sense your secret bloomings;
the rest will cut you at the stem.
But I will slice them from my tree
and graft into your bleeding veins
other branches from many nations.'
These revelations disturbed me beyond recognition;
I wanted to leave myself, my home, my life
and disappear leopardlike into the stippled hills
to find my self, my calm again.
Had I become a prophet of my own imagination?
Had I departed my fixed horizons?
My parents, sensing my inner angst, asked,
'Jesus, do you know who you are?
Your name was given to us by God
even before you came to our lives.
You are Israel's Savior and Deliverer.
You will rescue us from our enemies,
as spoke the Spirit and spirit-angels
in visions, dreams, and prophecies;
you will be the Lord's sword,
even if it pierces our hearts.'
Mary took my hand and said,
'I saw this when Gabriel came to me
and chose me, a virgin, to receive
the everlasting promised seed.
Ever since, I've psalmed my God in song:

Let my soul extol the Lord,
my spirit be glad for God my Savior,
who has shown compassion on his servant
who, for generations, will be called "blessed."
The divine Warrior has bared his strong Arm.
I treasure his potent sacred Name!
Though his mercy reaches all who revere him,

even generation after generation,
his hands are heavy against the proud,
whose high-mindedness he smears.
He topples the mighty from their thrones,
and lifts the lowly in his arms.
He feeds the hungry until they're full
and consigns the rich to emptiness.
Oh, now in mercy he's come to rescue Israel,
for he hasn't forgotten his promises
to Abraham and his seed forever.'

And Mary told me of further predictions
by angelic visits to our kinsfolk
beyond the buckthorned hills.
And then she recited Zechariah's poem
as if it had always been on her lips:

'Praise the Lord God of Israel
who has now visited his people
and come to redeem us, to save us
by giving us a mighty David!
Here is the fulfillment of the promise
spoken through his holy prophets—
that we would be rescued
from the enemies who hate us,
for God has not forgotten his covenant,
the oath he swore to Abraham:
that we would be freed
to serve our God fearlessly
in purity and righteousness
throughout all our living days.'

Then Mary said this was what Zechariah,
priest of God, promised his son:

'You are the prophet of God Most High,
the Lord's forerunner and pioneer
preparing the way for his parousia,
shouting as you go, ' "Your salvation is here!
It's coming from the coming Lord,
who shines as dawning sunbeams
on those who sit in falling shadows
waiting for death to be done." '

Like an ox moving the grinding stone,
I turned these prophecies over and over again
until my mind was weary and worn.
Was I the one chosen to rescue Israel
to deliver her from pagan dominion
then give her a new, unbloodied earth,
the hallowed land promised to our fathers?
I was no sword-wielding David,
no lionlike vengeance-seeking liberator.
To most, I was no more than a carpenter,
a well-read synagogue lector,
Joseph's son from Nazareth,
no Judas Maccabee, no Zion zealot,
no Savior brought in with wild winds.
But all the signs pointed to this:
my voices and their visions,
the prophecies and dreams;
yet I had no fierceness in my veins,
no malice for Rome, no hatred for pagans.
I despised only sin and what it did to men;
if I had a sword that could topple that,
I wouldn't halt to cut its head.

I wore down the rough hours with prayer

as scrollmakers rub hides to parchment.
I waited for an unmistakable finger
to quill the message, to point the way,
but there was no new writing on the scroll,
no beam falling quickly on my shoulders,
only smoldering flax and dwindling lamplight
by which I read the Scriptures over and over
long into gray Galilean nights.
Here and there in the tawny inscripted lines
I thought I saw my face before my time
in lives who had prophetic been:
Noah, the rescuer of a drowning world;
Joseph, the dreamer, saved to be savior;
Moses, the deliverer of the oppressed;
Samuel, God's child lent to be lent;
David of God's heart, branch of God's life,
dry ground root, shoot of King-Christ.
But then the visage disappeared
as in a mirror tainted and unclear.

 'Why, O God,' I shot at the vault,
'do so few realize I'm the One?
The magi know but snuck the secret
to the east in their empty treasure chests.
Zechariah's tongue, once unwound,
now lies silent in the muted grave,
and my sweet father Joseph knew
but the truth is buried with him.
Only my mother holds the revelation,
not my brothers, James, Joses, Jude, Simon,
nor even my precious sisters,
let alone the rest of our nation.
I know they won't believe a Nazarene;
no one knows I was Bethlehem-born.'

As the sun dragged the sky to its death every day
and the stars spattered the dark canvass,
I sensed a thickening veil between us;
the voice went mute, the visions waned,
His presence hushed and distant.
I told myself I was precociously insane
to have thought life was any different
for me than for the rest under the sun.
As the meetings dragged on, I'd stare
out the window at the blessed blue sky
and wonder why I hadn't heard or seen Him
in a long and silent while.
But since it was my task to learn the sacred text
and read it to the men on holy sabbath,
I studied the texts with heart and mind
and memorized the Scriptures through the hours
as I shaped yokes in the carpenter's shack.
I hardly left our Nazareth village,
except for a visit or two to Sepphoris;
once to Tyre on the Western Sea,
and once to Capernaum on Galilee.
I took the annual sojourns to Jerusalem
where we sang the happy Psalms of Ascents,
gloried in Zion's God, and celebrated Exodus.
But most of my days I endured routine
plying my trade and studying texts.
As I read and recited, I was often confounded
by passages evoking terror and dread
seizing those who neared the Holy God.
What was this potent awful Power
that moved men to such unholy fear?
Why was God so mysteriously withdrawn?
Why had no one ever seen his face and lived?

Each morning light led me to the synagogue
where I tried to read the Hebrew text
with Hebrew mind but found
I did not see it as they saw.
I was not drawn to the law of Moses
as much as to the sacred prophets,
those mystic poets who spoke my soul;
though their message was often obscure,
their unveiled thoughts made my world:
with David I psalmed sacred sweetness
(his songs were coverts from any tempest);
with Isaiah I envisioned new earth and heavens
where children were kings and lions lambs;
with Ezekiel I saw the living zoas
roving the earth with eyes and wings
and spirits moving as wheels within wheels,
lifting the Glory as it split the Temple;
with Jonah I fathomed depths of hell,
while Malachi put all things well when he exclaimed,
'To those who revere my Name
the Sun of Righteousness will arise
with healing in his wings.'

One dark morning of liquid dawn
I saw the daystar on my way to the synagogue
still soused with smoking flax.
Soon there was light enough to find the Torah
which, having not read for quite a while,
I unraveled to the beginning
and vocalized the seminal line,
'And God said let there be light.'
I was startled and afraid by what I heard;
this voice was not new to me.  It seemed to be mine.

I read it again and increased my fear;
could I have spoken in some earlier age
these very words written on this page?
And then I had the prescient sense
that I was there
when that inspiring voice
spun celestial spheres;
that I was there
when that sunburst rush
flashed a flood of stars
and lit the darkness poised in space;
that I was there
when that living breath
quickened dust and infused flesh;
that I was there,
I was there,
I was.

I kept this uncertain apocalypse to myself
but I knew I wasn't alone.
As I walked the paths around town
something told me heavily I'd never been,
that there was divine communion
between myself and another
whom I called Father and he called Son.
When I was not wrapped around bones,
spirit-free and roaming beyond sound or search,
everywhere and anywhere I was present
with the Father as his only One,
the impress of his essence,
the countenance of his presence.

When I returned to the synagogue
and read the Genesis script yet again,

the revelation got fuller and clearer
like the fattening of the moon,
until it became an undeniable heavenly sign:
I was there when it all began
when our Spirit brooded over deep seas
and penetrated darkness with winged rays
conquering chaos with flashing light.
Our word dispeled dismal dampness
as we separated the waters above
from those below with vaulted expanse.
We awoke earth from its frozen sleep
as it erupted with erect greens
from dark seas teeming with fish.
We arched the land with blessed air
filling birds, beasts, reptiles, insects
with breath and livingness and soul.
We scattered a million galaxies
like sand-grains on an ever-expanding beach,
then we gazed upon this plump universe
verved with vigor and hope and seed
and saw that everything was good:
chaos had been voided with light,
the damp void was flooded with life:
moving, making, commingling, shaping,
fluttering, flapping, leaping, clacking;
but there was still a certain emptiness
lingering in the liquid air;
for, of all the creatures under the sun,
nothing imagined or visaged us,
so we fashioned one from fecund soil
and breathed him into living soul.
This was the one who mirrored us;
this was the one we called Man!

Before I could absorb these lights,
I had another primeval flash:
I was there when we fashioned Woman,
the lustrous halo of all creation,
the envy of angels and desire of gods.
But she was paired for Adam only—
lip for lip, limb for limb, skin for skin,
and no one was permitted to pierce her
but he who was pierced to make his twin.
Yet there in the celestial court
of myriad angels, seraphim, and cherubim
of living zoa and exalted ones
was strange arousal and fierce desire
to explore her sensuousness
and impregnate her with unearthly fire.
When I became a man I knew this pull
(which was so strange to me then),
yet I did not yield to this sin
as did many of them in their fall,
when they entered earth's daughters
on their way to the holes of hell.

"And then - the sight still chills me -
I flashed to pre-chaotic past
of rememberances I would rather forget.
I envisioned a solitary prince high in the realm
whom the doxas called Lucifer, morning star;
he was far more resplendent than most
and could boast of having his own loyal host.
But he craved what I and the Father had,
self-existence and divine autonomy;
his envy took him away from us
to a distance never yet reconciled.
Denouncing the superior Sovereign,

he sought his own kingdom and dominion
which we confined between earth and heaven
where he ranges and rages on his way to ruin.
He now has another name, Satan, Opposer,
at war with himself, with us, and man
who, as the object of our affection,
became the target of his deception.
How sinister his mien, how sick his design
to make them like himself, not us,
gods cut off from paradise.
These recollections -no, revelations-
brought me to my knees with trembling.
I hadn't realized I was eternal.
I hadn't known I was His only Son,
that I had spawned creation's spring
and moaned the fall of human being.
I called on my Father in fear,
'What am I doing here as man?
Have I also fallen from glorious grace?
Was I cast to lower realms than Satan?
Oh Father, you must tell me
how I came to be who I am!"
Then a voice came to me from within,
'My son, you are what I am, but now as man.
The Spirit hovering over a chosen virgin
as clean and pure as heavenly canopy
covered her as a bridal tent,
impregnating her virgin womb
with heaven-sent sperm,
a miraculous event:
my Son
eternal Spirit
you became anthropic embryo
growing bones and brain

forming tiny fingers and lungs
to touch the earth we shaped
and breathe the air we made.
When you were born,
angels quaked, planets shook,
the glories stooped to look
at the rising *Anatole*.
Some magi rode from the east,
some shepherds stirred from the hills,
but no one else that clarion night
heard I had moved.
Scholars knowing Micah's prophecy
didn't salute the monarchic moment,
and Jerusalem was deaf to Bethlehem's tears
as babes were slaughtered for Herod's fears.
Egypt never knew you'd come and gone,
while Galilee stooped in shadowed sun
never imagined that holy light
would arise in their hollow eyes
while you were growing into man.'

The light faded, the voice ceased.
I could hardly rise from my knees,
these unveilings were too divine.
Could I believe that I, a creature,
had once been the Originator?
(Blasphemous? Preposterous?)
that I mortal was once immortal,
that I had lived when time was not?
I told myself I had wearied my flesh
with too much study of the text.
I had transposed what I read
to make it a description of myself.
And that's what most of you standing here

would have said and still might say today.
But now that I am deathless,
do you think I'm the making of a myth
or that I am Word fulfilled?"

No one answered.  No one dared to speak.
They knew he could read their thoughts
easier than any unscrolled book.

The wind had shifted to the east;
the sun was making its arched ascent,
its beams reflecting off the cedars,
while the Prophet began again
to speak his way into their hearts,
pioneering a forest of doubt,
axing stubs, unrooting gnarls, plowing
clods for sowing revolutionary thoughts:
"In the fifteenth year of Caesar Tiberius
while Pilate was ruler over Judea,
Herod Antipas governed Galilee,
and Annas with Caiphas were ruling priests,
another prophet-priest, Zechariah's son,
soused the land with sacred water
calling Israel everywhere to change their thought
and ready themselves for the coming kingdom.
The word spread as a wadi flood
throughout all of Judea and Galilee
that he was baptizing in the Jordan
and shouting with a prophet's warning:

'Prepare a path for the coming King.
Make a road straight for him.
Valleys fill, mountains level,
straighten the crooked, smooth the rough,

then you will see salvation of God!'

My spirit was stirred, the hour had come,
this was the voice I was waiting on.
I dropped the scrolls, left the yokes,
and headed for the Hebrew river.
As I stood with the crowd waiting immersion
and heard John proclaim, 'After me another comes
who is before me, because he's always been,'
I had no doubt that I was ready.
As I knelt before the Elijah-Baptizer,
his watery hands began to shake,
his sunbaked face rippled with waves of fear,
'Oh no,' he cried, 'I need *your* water and *your* fire!'
'Let it be for now,' I demanded. 'This is the way
for both of us to accomplish His righteousness.'
When I came up from the Jordan waters
God's glorious voice came dove-down to me,
'This is my Son, my delight and treasure.'
In that one instant the skies split open;
I saw my home, the God-lit heavens.
God's Spirit flooded, effused, embraced me
and thrust me beyond the Jordan waters
to the deadly empty wilderness.

I awoke from sleep as if it were a dream
sucked up by sirocco tongues.
I was deserted to my revelations
alone with the wind's moan,
no, not quite alone; the Spirit was with me
as the sun peeled the sky and skin.
Day after waterless day death came undisguised
scorpion-faced, snakeskin dry, tarantula-like
creeping toward me on its belly,

but I, like the hornet, knew where to sting.
Growling with Samson-strength
I shouted to the demonic lair,
'I will not yield to desert, to owl hoot and jackal howl.
I am not animal.  I make them. I turn my thoughts to food,
and drink the Spirit pushing me further into deprivation!
I must keep moving, a fugitive of lust
that will not find me wilderness.
Angels, you know nothing of this,
but some of you transgressing your realm
want to battle your fate and doom.
Come, Satan, try to kingdom-come me
with promises of glory surreal!
Spread your sumptuous realms before me,
a moveable feast on a banquest table
by Greeks, Persians, Medes, Romans,
with their wisdom, women, and wine.
I desire nothing from them or you who claim
to be my food if I bow down to you,
for I in this thin frontier
suck words from sticks and stone;
they're honey to me from a lion slain!'
　　　'But you can take the fall, survive the leap,'
the transmogrified angel said.
'You're God's Son, His precious one;
He'll send his angels to catch you,
to fetch you before you plunge too far.'
　　　'No, I will not tempt my God,' I shouted back,
'like you who have a wounded head
because you pushed the edge.
Disappear in your tempest!
I will not kneel to your mastery.
I am free to serve my Elohim.'
　　　'For now, I'll leave,' the foul angel howled,

'but I'll return for your dark hour.'

And just as I was enjoying my conquest,
I was taken by Spirit through Hades' gates,
where I saw the battle-scarred and wounded,
the maimed and marred and half-insane
and those who bent delusion.
(Abraham's bosom was still a place of rest
for beggars, bums, and bastards,
for hellshot minds and tortured souls
escaping Gehenna and Armageddon.)
But for the most, I saw thronging ghosts
trying desperate to storm Hades' gate
as if it were the stone on an ancient tomb.
'No exit! no exit!' they screamed above the wail
of tortured demons thrashing chains
trying to escape Tartarian pits of slime.
Imprisoned angels had lost their grip.
Whores, pimps and freaks clung to each other's ghosts
as they fell headlong in a vanishing abyss.
Mangled, crazed, tortured souls, crippled, broken, hapless folk,
those who used to be the glorious rich and famed the earth
crawled all fours to the door where darkness never broke.
As they peered in, they saw it was no place at all,
for hell was their fire and nothingness their hell.
I moaned and groaned for these anguished souls
who had gone to the devil without him going, too.

When I returned from this Spirit-vision,
I rinsed my mind of evil and determined
to squeeze every torturous drop from hell.
Wrung out from the desert's press
and cleansed of sinking appetites,
I called to Yahweh and let my spirit yell:

'I am hungry for God,
could eat a mouthful of angels
and feel most divine
except for this skin called desire
which I have conquered
and will pummel again!
What pain to become what I never was!
I had emptied my glory
and filled my being
with human being
and all that meant
of suffering man.
And now I have taken Satan on,
who used to be lovely and fair
but now has to pretend
that he is more than wasted
in a wasted kingdom.
I am warrior, after all,
I fought with flesh, I battled air
and vanquished both with spirit!'

The other angels witnessing this from afar
were stunned that I a son of man
had conquered one of the elohim
who had stolen glory from God
and thought that I, who had relinquished
this majesty with inscrutable willingness,
might redeem it for his place.
The angels swooped down like ravens
one after one, a thousand of them,
bringing me Edenic wine and victory cakes.
Refreshed, infused and extoled,
I was ready to run the world
with God's good gospel news,

which I shouted to the lands
of the east, west, north, and south:
'I've conquered him who made you slaves
of flesh and freed you from your foe!'

On the way back from the wrinkled desert,
passing junipers, brooms, and brambles,
I was startled by wild sounds
of the wilderness gone wet and wadi:
ravines flashing with surging water,
resurrected frogs still shrouded in mud
croaking through the cracks of night,
coyotes howling moonside of lightning,
hungry for vermin aroused by rainbursts,
owlscreech stunning the snakes hunting mice,
as all was soaked with thunder.
I crawled into a cave cliffside to the salt sea
as dead as ever, even with a flash of fresh stream;
it was dry inside, dry-mouth dry
and old as an Egyptian coffin.
I slept embalmed in long strong dreams
of sun and song and gleaming heaven
and awoke to torrent streams of light
penetrating my eyelids, lumining the cave
where, to my surprise, I saw a slender vase
standing cherublike in a hollow niche,
looking as much like a scroll container
as ever I'd seen in my genizah.
Poking its head above the brim,
the scroll begged me come and open.

My eyes fell on Isaiah's inscripted lines
as he told my story without having been.
I could hardly hold my mind from racing ahead.

What was this I read?!

A light would arise on the way
of the sea, beyond the Jordan
in Galilee of the Gentiles
to shine on those who walked in death
to chase their shadows and light the path
that leads to God and righteousness.
Virgin-conceived, he would be called Immanuel,
Wonderful Counselor, Mighty God, Prince of Peace!

Why had I not seen this before?
Why had no rabbi ever known?
As I read on, I couldn't help but laugh:
The eyes of the blind will open,
the ears of the deaf unstop,
the lame will leap like spring deers,
and the tongue of the dumb will sing,
for water will gush in the deserts
and stream through the arid wastes;
dry ground will become unparched
as the thirsty land will spring fresh;
the dens where the jackals used to hide
will become plots of reed and papyri
bending in the eastern breeze.

As I read on in the arid lair,
I was quietened by the Spirit I heard
as I listened to my Father's voice
speak the pages of my life:

'Here is my servant whom I uphold,
my chosen one, my heart's delight.
I have drenched him in my Spirit;

he will judge the world with fairness,
not by raising his voice in the streets;
he does not crush the broken reed
or snuff the smoldering flax.
He will not grow weary
and he will not be crushed
until he has kingdomed my earth.'

My Father who spread out the heavens,
fashioned earth, gave breath and spirit
to all who walk upon the soil, said to me,

'I have grasped you by the hand and shaped you
to be a covenant to my people
and a light to all the nations
to open their long-blind eyes
and free the captives from their chains.
I will reveal fresh events to you;
before they appear I will tell you their truth.'

As I kept reading the prophet, I was astounded
that he was speaking of me when he said,

'Yahweh called me when I was in the womb,
before I was born he uttered my name.
He made my mouth a piercing sword
and hid me in the shadow of his hand.
He formed me into a penetrating arrow
and concealed me in his quiver.'

'That's why I was hidden so long!'
I exclaimed to the wind whirling through the cave.
'I was formed in the womb to be His servant,
to bring Israel back to their God,

to be the light for all the world,
a savior for the pagans and obscure!'
Oh, how I was gladdened by these words.
But then a troubling urge pushed me
to unravel the scroll a little more.

This is what I read aloud as I sat
at cave's edge looking to the east,

'Yahweh has given me a servant's tongue
to know how to comfort the weak and weary.
He has given me an ear to listen to him
and I have not resisted.
I gave my back to those who whipped me,
my cheeks to those who plucked my beard.
I didn't turn my face from being spat upon,
for the Lord himself, my help, is near.
That is why I set my face like a flint
and know I will never be put to shame.'

'Am I… am I… am I that man?' I yelled to the rocks.
'Am I that servant of whom Isaiah spoke
he was so inhumanly disfigured
he was no longer a man,
nations were astonished, people aghast—
to whom was the Arm of the Lord revealed?
He was a sapling, a root in desert-dry ground
with no form or beauty to attract.
He was despised, the lowest of men,
a man of sorrows, suffering pain;
we turned away our gaze from him,
yet he was the one bearing our griefs,
carrying our sorrows to their death.
While we thought he was being punished

by God and scourged with divine afflictions,
he was being wounded for our sins
and deeply crushed for our guilt;
by his bruises we are healed,
for God laid on him the sins of the world.'

My hands trembled, my spirit sank;
too weak to hold the scroll anymore
I caved to the floor and moaned,
'O Lord, no, Father, this can't be me.
Tell me this is another yet to come.
Am I not the glorious Savior, the advent King?
I couldn't be a sacrifice for sin.'
No answer came, just more wind
circling through the corners of the cave.

When I returned home to Nazareth,
there were no shouts of praise,
no acclamations for my conquest,
there was, as always had been,
the rocking, the reading, the religious
breathing and contemplation of sayings
in our sober sacred synagogue.
As was the sabbath custom,
I was handed Isaiah's scroll,
wherein I easily found the script and read,
'The Lord's Spirit is upon me,
he has anointed me, of all men,
to give the poor good news.
He has sent me to proclaim
that the captives will be freed,
that the blind will finally see,
that the oppressed will be released
from all their oppressive dread,

for the time of grace has come.'

Then I looked at all of them,
my friends and family of Nazareth,
and proclaimed in the firmest voice,
'Today, this day, this Scripture is fulfilled.
It has come to pass as surely as you heard.'

When I rolled up Isaiah's scroll,
all eyes in the synagogue
were fastened on my face
marvelling at my gracious words,
astounded that a native could say
the scripture had actually taken place.
They hadn't heard the heavenly voice
tell the Spirit-effused man,
 'You are my lovely Son;
my heart delights in you.'
Those Nazarenes only knew
I was Joseph's son, a carpenter,
I couldn't be the chosen One.
'No,' their eyes glared, 'you can't open
prison gates, closed mouths, stopped ears;
you can't fix our broken hearts
or spring the jubilee year.
You're one of us, a mere man,
our desperate kin.
We have words to keep us sane.
But show us again Capernaum
and we might believe in you.'

'My friends,' I told them,
'God's word lives beyond the book,
he moves beyond our kind

to such as Naaman the Syrian
whose leprosy left his skin
and to such as the widow of Zarephath
boiling poisonous sticks.'
Enraged, they threw conscience away
and would have flung me from the cliff,
but I passed through their midst
headed for a greater death,
and a life of giving health
to a humanity sick of itself.

As I left to go back to Capernaum
I said to myself, 'No prophet
has a home in the hearts of his own.'
I knew those hillfolk Nazarenes,
who saw me as a yoke-mender
with rough hands, stale sweat, and zeal,
wouldn't believe I was Spirit-soaked,
heaven-sent to free them from their pains.
In truth, there are some of you now
sitting here who still hardly believe.
But I knew there'd be those who worked the waters
whom I could draw and pull and catch;
they were men of different mind.
Some had been with John, most I never met.
I came to two of them on this sunstreaked lake
early in the morning dawn.
I could tell they were weary of the night.
'No, I won't catch the perch,' I said to myself,
though I saw them swimming in opaque pools
thin as bread, thick in swirling schools
near the port side of their skiff
that had crossed the lake again and again
following the full-masted moon

until there was nothing but vacant sky and sun.
'Cast the net now and you will catch!' I shouted.
A sudden surge, bend, and silver flash
flushed these drained fishermen
who drew the catch to surface
and now saw what I had seen
deep in green Genesareth,
encircled, enclosed, unaware but known
they were chosen, drawn and snatched.

By now, the sun had crowned and crested
over the Galilean hills and sea;
the trees glimmered in the brightness.
The five hundred had been so enraptured
by this epiphany, time was nothing as it passed.
Jesus ate some fresh fish and bread,
and encouraged them all to do the same.
Then he asked the Eleven to come sit with him,
while he continued to reveal his thoughts.
Turning to Peter, Jesus asked,
"Do you remember, even after that miraculous catch,
you weren't sure I was worth the sacrifice?
What was it made you rise and follow?"
Peter started to answer then stopped,
as the Prophet continued on:
"I called other men, all of whom are here now,
except for one, my grim betrayer,
who threw away his soul for silver.
Matthew, you took your quill and codex,
erased taxes and inscribed it with my words.
Simon, you abandoned your zealous patriots
and grabbed my message as your sword.
Thomas, you doubted until you saw for yourself
that nails and spear can't kill your God.

Philip, you wanted to see the Father,
and when you did, you saw my face.
James, you said you could drink my cup—
you will do so, and be the first.
Peter, when you were young,
you dressed yourself and wandered as you willed,
but when you grow old, others will gird you
and take you where you the trees are cruel.
And John, you saw the Baptist point to the Lamb
then followed me, even to the crooked hill,
while all the rest abandoned me in death."

At this, all the disciples were downcast;
no one dared to lift the head or speak.
" 'Don't fear death or death's demise!
Live! my brothers. Live, my sisters,
as fierce conquerers of the grave!'
the Prophet exclaimed.
Don't you remember, Andrew and James,
Philip and Thomas, that sad day
when the funeral rolled out of town
like a tear down a hollow cheek
and everyone moved slowly lamenting, grieving,
daring not to look at the widow's sorrow
who clung to the bier of her only son,
when suddenly another procession
from another direction stopped them on the way;
it was I who came and took her anguish
when I touched the coffin and gave her back her life!

There were others I touched
who felt the power of force
infusing quick therapy:
the blind crying for mercy

received their sight from David's son,
lepers leaped and laughed
when the pale ghost left their skin,
the mute spoke in perfect tongues
when they heard my living word,
and broken-spirited folk wept
when the physician fixed their sins.
My speech startled them, my stories allured;
though they didn't understand,
they knew I preached the real and wanted more.
My liquid lore unthirsted them,
my parables stuffed them with bread;
though they went away wondering,
they went away fed,
and always they would come back
sparrows to the golden grain,
so I would speak life to them again.
My teachings revolutionized their minds
as to who was going to find the kingdom—
the spiritually poor, not the rich
the hungry and thirsty for justice
the meek, who'll inherit a new earth
(not the arrogant and dominant lords)
the pure in heart, who will see their God
the peacemakers, not warmongers
all these will be divinely blessed
and persecuted for my Name.

I, the parable-maker, the story master,
unlocked the kingdom with the keys of my lips;
for those who had hearts to enter
it was not difficult to find.
But I stupified the riddled minds
I garbled words for those without ears,

for they would never understand
mysteries hidden from the world's foundation -
that I had come to enlighten all nations
and to give every soul eternal salvation,
not just to Israel or Palestine,
but further, much further, beyond the islands
I would drop the sacred seeds.

Everywhere I journeyed,
from Galilee to Samaria,
from Sidon to Jerusalem,
I was swarmed with multitudes
of multitudes thicker than the plagues.
I thought aloud what no one heard,
'The feeble crowd me, their strong thoughts
overwhelm me. They surround God
and swarm him unashamedly with need,
as they desperately cling
for anything from His kindness
to see them through another troubled day.
That is why I taught them to pray:

'Our Father who inhabits heaven
your Name alone is sacred.
May you kingdom earth with heaven
and fulfill your heart's desire.
Give us daily the sustaining bread
and forgive us all our debts and sins
as we forgive our debtors.
Don't lead us down temptation's path;
from every evil rescue us.'

The people listened to my words
but didn't comprehend that the kingdom

was among them in the potent Son of Man.
The demons knew and shrieked in terror,
'God's Son, spare us till the last hour!'
How many did I rescue from demonic force?
Legions of beleagured bullied men
and yet your religious leaders from Jerusalem
audaciously, even blasphemously, charged
I was working by Beelzebul's power.
(This sin won't ever be forgiven them.)
I was not a thaumaturgist or exorcist,
but that's what the masses thought
who came like wind from every direction
as word of my powers got out.
The Syro-Phoenican woman
with a draining flood of blood
tapped my power for cure.
The desperate Roman centurion
with a dear servant dying at home
begged me command his healing
and it happened as I spoke.
The parents of a little daughter
grieving death, along with all the rest,
saw me raise her, saying, "Talitha cum."
John, James, Peter - you remember -
you alone were with me then.
Always, everywhere around me
there was need and desperate want.
I changed water to wine,
fed multitudes from a few broken fish and rye,
and stilled the storm of a thousand cries.
But there was not enough of me,
never enough of me to go around,
and most failed to read the signs.

I would escape the rush of desperate souls
and retreat to the hushed wilderness
where I slipped into prayer and vision
and passionate longings for my former life,
with achings for a body of another kind
without sinews tendons nerves and skin
captive to the pain of aging.
When I was young I climbed the hills
with swift wings it seemed
but in later years I tired and panted
even on my way up to Jerusalem.
'Is this what it is to be human?' I moaned.
'To slowly lose form and face
to turn ugly gnarly and sad
to feel the dying before you're dead?
Oh, God, the mortal curse falls on us all!
I must break it, forsake it, cut it,
take it to the meanest hell.
Oh my God and never-dying Father,
how could you put eternal in their hearts
when they funeral to their end?
But I am different. I will lose my bones,
return to Spirit and spirit home.'

The Father stopped me mid-prayer,
'No, my Son, you have become man
to be man forever. There's no return
to pristine glory except as human
and that depends on your perfection.
All creation groans for this,
but Satan will ruin you if he can.'

'No,' I shouted, 'never to speed again
as spirit pure, as bright effulgent sunbeam

41

but to move as slow as bones.
How could I have ever acquiesced
to take into myself human flesh
with all its naturalness and sin -
and I must never ever give in -
no, not once, or I am destined for dust
like all the rest - tell me it's a lie!'
But no word came in the silent wind.
'O God, I knew it, I am forever this.
I am forever and always man.'

As I returned from desert prayer
and entered the Sharon valley,
I caught sight of harvested vineyards
stripped to the branch of every grape
and grainfields threshed to stubble
where nothing was left but trampled gleanings;
this was clearer than any beaming vision,
more potent than any angel-sent word:
'Life given is life taken.
That's why I'm body, that's why man.
I'm the grain falling into earth
to multiply a million births.'

Then I came to Capernaum again
and began to teach in their synagogue,
where a huge crowd had gathered
for more miraculous bread
not even because they'd seen a sign.
I'll tell you again what I preached then,
'I am manna dropped from heaven;
I'm God's food freshly slain.
Come, eat the body, drink the blood
of the broken open Son of Man.

Don't miss the Spirit of my message,
for this is life to those who come.'
Most of you abandoned me then
to the desolation of your own conceptions;
yes, the fervent expectation of revolution
weighed heavily, not heavenly, on my frame.
How could I dethrone your imaginations?
I was not another savior from Rome.
And the leaders, still following ancient Moses,
as if he were leading Israel to promised land
like the moon pulling stars through darkness,
tempted me to push the heavens for a sign.
But I was destined for one singular event
to be a temple raized and raised again,
the glorified, uplifted Son of Man!"

Until now, no one dared to speak,
epecially those who had been deserters.
But Peter with his usual boldness queried,
'Does this mean you will make the kingdom
by restoring David's fallen tents?'
 'My dear brother,' Jesus replied,
'don't you remember when I went to Jerusalem
during Tabernacles' feast and proclaimed,
' "Come drink of me, the smitten rock,
I'm living water for all who thirst." '
In saying this, I spirit spoke,
my spirit gushing from the broken stone,
flowing everlasting with life satisfying.
Come taste eternal sweetness now
as I quench your thirsty souls—
this is kingdom filling you.
And don't you recall the Baptist's words:
'God can raise stones to be Abraham's sons.'?

The temple was once God's glorious home;
it will soon become desolate rubble
for they rejected the Father's Son
who would have gathered them together
as a mother hen collects her own.
But the glory has left Israel, as Ezekiel spoke,
for the leaders fashioned religion into their idol
turning it to Mammon, a den of thieves,
taking worship from Yahweh, they stole his praise
and turned away the desire of nations.
I sacrileged Judean Jewry, toppled
their pillars stacked heavy with laws,
ripped off the yoke, lightened burden.
Looking for another Moses, they missed
the Prophet and killed his message.
Zion is a fruitless vine, a figless tree;
not a cluster of grapes or single fig
to satisfy the harvestpicker's taste.
I plowed hard hearts, planted seed,
but the grain died in parched ground
yielding nothing but wild wind.
The time will soon come, O Jerusalem,
when you will be rubbled, stones plowed under,
a tangled thicket for foxes and wolves—
they will howl for your loss and my hunger.

Turning to the multitude of disciples he shouted,
"You are the kingdom, my temple,
stones raised with me from the rubble.
You are my extension, my body, expression—
you who witnessed God's glory
secretly dwelling in human being.
You will seed the world with my message,
for you have seen the God-man, touched him,

beheld him, heard him, and known him.
Even now you see the nailprints in my hands,
the piercing, and whippings on my back.
I took on death and returned again.
You shouldn't have doubted my power
to pass through Hades and reappear
visible still physical yet transformed.
But the passage was pain and wailing;
in those days before I took the cross
I felt Job's anguish and disgust,
the unfairness of flesh, moan of bones,
the knowing I could be spirit again
but had to inhabit a cloistered tomb.
I so human, so very human felt
as I rinsed my thoughts in blood,
bowing to my destiny with some regret:
how cruel and cursed to wear this corpse
to carry each man's death to a criminal's crucifix.
Who of you believed I was death-headed?
None of you swallowed the Jonah sign,
even though I told you three times
I would be despised, crucified, and rise.
Mary knew my hour was near.
Sensing the moment, seizing the last touch
she incensed the party at Lazarus' house
with myrrh from a broken heart,
a welcomed odor to her lover
for it covered a noxious stench:
the obnoxious waste of the dead
for whom cost was counted more than love.

I anguished over you in those days
after you saw Lazarus raised
and heard the glorious hosannas,

the victory shouts to David's son
in the palm-strewn streets of Jerusalem.
How could you not feel that we had come
to the kingdom promised by the prophets?
But I knew differently and grimly
that the Shepherd would be smitten
and you scattered to every sad imagination."

He turned his gaze on the Eleven sitting close to him
and spoke solemn to all assembled there,
"My last meal together with the Twelve
was heaven mingled with hell—
heaven, for I knew I would drink again
with them the wine of paradise;
hell, because I was being betrayed
by one of my own, devil-seduced.
My feelings for them were these thoughts:
'Space separates us now;
I am close to them but far away;
these ragged men fill places in my heart.
When we are apart what will they feel?
Do they know I will Spirit them?
I, who have been by their side these three years.
So I told them, as I tell you all now again,
'I will give you another Comforter,
the Parakletos, Encourager and Teacher.
You know who he is. It's not mystery.
He is with you now and will indwell you
and you in him as branches in the vine.
Let my Spirit live in you
and I will make you join the divine.'

Once our meal and psalming was done,
I was alone in Gethsemane. I was oil pressed,

squeezed to the last drop of faith,
my spirit groaning desperate prayer:
'Father, who will believe I was heaven-sent
that I breathed as God in foreverness,
as they are about to see me die as naked flesh?
Must I make this sacrifice?
Hasn't it been enough
that I was Messiah misunderstood,
thought to be born in Galilee
an unlearned and rebellious man?
Must I be nailed to the crooked tree?'

Then the Father spoke to me,
'You know your destiny and hour.
No more "hosannas" and "blessed David."
They will shout, "Blasphemy!  Away with him!"
not knowing that the Son of man
as their Son of sorrows
is taking all that's human,
feeling all that's pain,
tasting death for every man,
for every death you came.
I cannot take the cup from you;
you must swallow every drop.'

Nothing was so grievous as knowing destiny
and not being able to move there quickly.
The hours dragged on like fishless days
at sea under a sunless signless sky,
while I pryed the vaulted sphere
under the tangled olive tree:
'What if, O God, I am left limp
in Hades' palid dampness
tortured by the nothingness of waste,

47

never raised to see your glorious face
to take my honored place with you?
What if it has all been a strong lie,
a casting of the wrong die, a falling
from your eternal favor, a change of mind,
and I am left behind to maggot,
to be forgotten, a failed experiment?
(If the fire doesn't melt me, my flames will!)
Forgive me, I am speaking out of mind,
out of place. Of course, this was designed.
But why must I, perfect from the core,
have to become a perfected pioneer?
I have felt sin and never once given in.
But to taste death and swallow it!
Is that fair for me, who am divine,
to absorb the mortal into my soul,
a sponge soaking sour wine,
when I, to evil, have been a stone?
Cast me away, my God, from this earth
toss me before I take the curse,
for I may never return sane or soul.
I may disappear a shade, a ghost
into the nether chaos of nothingness.
Let me not become abyss
as I suck this hideous sop.
Let me sip paradise and imbibe your praise.
Give notice to the craving grave:
'I will not be its food!'

And then
it happened:
the Sanhedrin oven
blazed with evil;
their plot smoldered

through the night.
In the morning
it broke out
a raging fire.
I was hunted
by Caiphas,
betrayed
by Judas
with a kiss,
condemned
a criminal
by Pilate,
scourged
by Rome,
forced
to carry
a beam
to the stake.
A tablet
stating
my crime
was fastened
to the pole,
'King of the Jews'
it said.
I a prisoner
was nailed
naked
to the cross
through
my wrists
and feet.
I was raised
and fixed

to the pole.
Hours passed.
Dice were
thrown
for my cloak.
I refused
drugged wine.
Mary groaned
with John her son
as they watched me
suffer like a worm.

I heard
the scribes
chief priests
and elders jibe,
'Save yourself
if you're God's Son.
Come down
from the cross
if you're our King!
Then we'll see
and believe.'
The soldiers
mocked me too
as did one
of the crucified.
But the other rebel
dying moaned,
'Remember me,
when you enter
your kingdom.'
And beneath me
I heard a centurion

in prayer,
'Oh, God's Son,
rescue me from who I am
and what we've done.
I want to die with you
and come back again
as though the ghost
of my former self
had been hung
and I was pardoned.'
I cried to my Father
and gave my spirit up—
it was finished
completed, done."

The multitude gathered on that Galilean hill
was still and tearful and silent
as all were crushed with guilt.
"Why," each agonized, "why alone
did he die for my sins?
I should have gone with him,
to Jerusalem, to Gethsemane, to Calvary."
"No," Jesus interrupted, "I had to go alone,
for only the Son of Man could do what I have done.
Now go to Jerusalem where you will see me
ascend to my pristine glory.
Witness me to a vacant world;
be my body as I Spirit move."

The wind stirred as the sun disappeared out of sight,
lengthening their thoughts like shadows.
It was hard for them to grasp
they had seen the risen One
and touched the Godman with their hands.

But the stirring of their spirits told them different.
One by one they got up and left
their sea, their sense, their nothingness
and followed the only path to God
which must be traveled from heart to head.


## EPILOGUE

A butterfly fluttered in the tall wind
sprouting monarchial wings
thin as angels but substantial—
the corporeal color of heaven unfurling,
as it floated between the longleafed boxtrees
through cedars, oaks, and cypress
moving majestically easy—
transfigured, fair, and nature's master—
flitting wings papyrus sheer
transparent, bloodred, untorn
unaware of its sway.
In quick season it would pilgrim
the bends and ascend its way
to the gathering of myriads more
yet to come, each alone, on wing, on wind
to rejuvenated trees and mountains
soaked in sacred sun and orange.